TEXTING

DICTIONARY

OF

ACRONYMS

LOL...............Laugh Out Loud

BFF ....Best Friends Forever

PLOS ....Parents Looking Over Shoulder

NISM.............Need I Say More

THIRD EDITION

Randall C. Manning ©2012

C G Publishing LLC   Copyright 2012

www.cgpublishinginc.com

Third Edition

OVER **1,200** ACRONYMS AND SYMBOLS

Thank you for purchasing the Texting Dictionary of Acronyms.

The newest language being formed is the language of texting. Sentences and phrases are now compressed into acronym and symbol forms. This book contains over 1,200 acronyms and symbols used by the mainstream texting world.

As this is an ever changing language, some phrases may or may not be omitted or added in future editions. Please feel free to contact publisher at citgraph@embarqmail.com to make comments or recommendations for future editions.

Please visit our website: www.cgpublishinginc.com to purchase other great books or get the latest **app version** of the Texting Dictionary Of Acronyms.

Original Copyright 2009

Randall C. Manning, Author/Publisher

Ronda L. Manning, Editor

ISBN 978-0-615-32930-7

Printed in the U.S.A.

Copyright © 2012 Randall C. Manning
C G Publishing LLC

TEXTING
DICTIONARY
OF
ACRONYMS

Copyright © 2012 Randall C. Manning
C G Publishing LLC

Printed in the U.S.A.

Copyright © 2012 Randall C. Manning
C G Publishing LLC

Original Copyright 2009

Randall C. Manning, Author/Publisher

Ronda L. Manning, Editor

TABLE OF CONTENTS

!......................	I have a comment
:<>	Amazed
o:-)	Angel smiley
:-II	Angry
:-X	Big Kiss
*:-)	Clown
%-)	Confused
d8:)	Cool Guy
:'-(...................	Crying
:e	Disappointed
:-|	Disgusted
o-&-<	Doing nothing
:-).....	Drooling face
:*)	Drunk smiling face
&:-)	From a person with curly hair
#:-)	From a person with matted hair
|-)	Getting tired, asleep
:-, ...	Hmmmm..., smirking
O-S-<	In a hurry
:-*	Kiss
:-D	Laughing
<3	Love Heart
:o	Ooooh!!", shocked
O-G-<	Pointing to self

@--<-->	red rose (aaaahhh..)
:-(	Sad
:-@	Screaming
8-)	Sunglasses face
:-O	Surprised/shocked
:-P	Tongue in cheek
:-&	Tongue tied
:-))	Very Happy
;-)	Winking
02	Your (or my) two cents worth
121	One to one
1337	Elite -or- leet
143	I love you
14AA41	One for All and All for One
182	I hate you
20	Location
2B or not 2B	To Be Or Not To Be
2BZ4UQT	Too Busy For You Cutey
2G4BG	Too Good To Be Forgotten
2GBT	Too Good To Be True
2moro	Tomorrow
2nite	Tonight
2U2	To You Too
4	for
404	I haven't a clue

411	Information
420	Marijuana
459	I love you
4COL	For Crying Out Loud
4EAE	For Ever And Ever
4ever	Forever
4NR	Foreigner
4U	For You
831	I Love You
86	Out of, over, to get rid of, or kicked out
9	Parent is watching
911	Emergency Call Me
99	Parent is no longer watching
<3	Heart
?	I have a question
@TEOTD	At The End Of The Day

A

A?	Eh?
A/S/L/P	Age/Sex/Location/Picture
A3	Anyplace, Anywhere, Anytime
AAAAA	American Association Against Acronym Abuse

AAF	As A Friend
AAK	Asleep At Keyboard
AAMOF	As A Matter Of Fact
AAMOI	As A Matter Of Interest
AAR	At Any Rate
AAR8	At Any Rate
AAS	Alive And Smiling
AATK	Always At The Keyboard
AAYF	As Always, Your Friend
ABITHIWITTB	A Bird in The Hand is Worth Two in The Bush
ABT2	About To
ACD	Alt Control Delete
ACE	Access Control Entry
ACK	Acknowledgement
ACORN	A Completely Obsessive Really Nutty Person
ADAD	Another Day Another Dollar
ADBB	All Done Bye Bye
ADIP	Another Day in Paradise
ADN	Advanced Digital Network -or- Any Day Now
ADR	Address
AEAP	As Early As Possible

AFAGAY	A Friend As Good As You
AFAHMASP	A Fool And His Money Are Soon Parted
AFAIAA	As Far As I Am Aware
AFAIC	As Far As I'm Concerned
AFAICS	As Far As I Can See
AFAICT	As Far As I Can Tell
AFAIK	As Far As I Know
AFAIR	As Far As I Remember
AFAIU	As Far As I Understand
AFAIUI	As Far As I Understand It
AFAP	As Far As Possible
AFAYC	As Far As You're Concerned
AFC	Away From Computer
AFINIAFI	A Friend In Need Is A Friend Indeed
AFJ	April Fools Joke
AFK	Away From Keyboard -or- A Free Kill
AFPOE	A Fresh Pair Of Eyes
AFZ	Acronym Free Zone
AGB	Almost Good Bridge
AGKWE	And God Knows What Else
AIAMU	And I'm A Monkey's Uncle

AIGHT	All Right
AIH	As It Happens
AIMB	As I Mentioned Before
AIMP	Always In My Prayers
AISB	As I Said Before
AISE	As I Said Earlier
AISI	As I See It
AITR	Adult In The Room
AKA or a.k.a.	Also Known As
ALAP	As Late As Possible
Alcon	All Concerned
ALOL	Actually Laughing Out Loud
ALOTBSOL	Always Look On The Bright Side Of Life
ALTG	Act Locally, Think Globally
AMAP	As Many As Possible -or- As Much As Possible
AMBW	All My Best Wishes
AML	All My Love
AMRMTYFTS	All My Roommates Thank You For The Show
ANFAWFOS	And Now For A Word From Our Sponsor

ANFSCD	And Now For Something Completely Different
ANGB	Almost Nearly Good Bridge
AOAS	All Of A Sudden
AOB	Abuse Of Bandwidth
AON	Apropos Of Nothing
AP	Apple Pie
AS	Another Subject
ASAMOF	As A Matter Of Fact
ASAP	As Soon As Possible
ASAYGT	As Soon As You Get This
ASL	Age/Sex/Location
ASLMH	Age/Sex/Location/Music/Hobbies
ATB	All The Best
ATC	Any Two Cards
ATSL	Along The Same Line
ATST	At The Same Time
ATW	All the Web -or- Around the Web
ATWD	Agree That We Disagree
AWC	After While, Crocodile
AWGTHTGTTA	Are We Going To Have To Go Through This Again
AWHFY	Are We Having Fun Yet?
AWLTP	Avoiding Work Like The Plague

AWNIAC .... All We Need Is Another Chair
AWOL .... Absent Without Leave
AWTTW .... A Word To The Wise
AYC .... Aren't You Clever -or- Aren't
.... You Cheeky
AYCE .... All You Can Eat
AYFT .... Are You Free Tonight
AYK .... As You Know
AYOR .... At Your Own Risk
AYSOS .... Are You Stupid Or Something
AYTMTB .... And You're Telling Me This Because
AYV .... Are You Vertical?

B

B&F .... Back and Forth
B/C .... Because
B4 .... Before
B4N .... Bye For Now
B4U .... Before You
B4YKI .... Before You Know It
BAG .... Busting A Gut
BAK .... Back At Keyboard
BARB .... Buy Abroad but Rent in Britain
BAU .... Business As Usual

BB	Be Back
BB4N	Bye Bye for Now
BBB	Bye Bye Babe -or-
	Boring Beyond Belief
BBBG	Bye Bye Be Good
BBF	Big Boy Foods
BBFBBM	Body By Fisher, Brains By Mattel
BBFN	Bye Bye for Now
BBIAB	Be Back In A Bit
BBIAF	Be Back In A Few
BBIAS	Be Back In A Sec
BBIAW	Be Back In A While
BBL	Be Back Later
BBN	Bye Bye Now
BBR	Burnt Beyond Repair
BBS	Be Back Soon -or-
	Bulletin Board Service
BBSD	Be Back Soon Darling
BBSL	Be Back Sooner or Later
BBT	Be Back Tomorrow
BBW	Big Beautiful Woman
BC	Because
BCBG	Bon Chic Bon Genre -or-
	Belle Cu Belle Geulle

BCBS	Big Company, Big School
BCNU	Be Seeing You
BCOZ	Because
BD	Big Deal -or- Baby Dance -or- Brain Drain
BDBI5M	Busy Daydreaming Back In 5 Minutes
BDC	Big Dumb Company -or- Big Dot Com
BDN	Big Darn Number
BEG	Big Evil Grin
BF	Boyfriend -or- Best Friend
BFF	Best Friends Forever
BFFN	Best Friends For Now
BFFTTE	Best Friends Forever Til The End
BFN	Bye For Now
BHAG	Big Hairy Audacious Goal
BHG	Big Hearted Guy -or- Big Hearted Girl
BHL8	Be Home Late
BHOF	Bald Headed Old Fart
BHPH	Buy Here Pay Here
BI5	Back In Five
BIBI	Bye Bye
BIBO	Beer In, Beer Out

BIF	Basis In Fact -or- Before I Forget
BIL	Brother-In-Law -or- Boss Is Listening
BION	Believe It Or Not
BIOYE	Blow It Out Your Ear
BIOYIOP	Blow It Out Your I/O Port
BIOYN	Blow it Out Your Nose
BITCH	Basically In The Clear Homey
BITD	Back In The Day
BJJDI	Billy Joel Just Drove In
BKA	Better Known As
BL	Belly Laughing
BLBBLB	Back Like Bull, Brain Like Bird
BM	Byte Me
BMGWL	Busting My Gut With Laughter
BMOF	Bite Me Old Fart
BMT	Before My Time
BNDN	Been Nowhere Done Nothing
BNF	Big Name Fan
BO	Bug Off -or- Body Odor
BOBFOC	Body Off Baywatch, Face Off Crimewatch
BOCTAAE	But Of Course There Are Always Exceptions
BON	Believe it Or Not

BOTEC	Back Of The Envelope Calculation
BOTOH	But On The Other Hand
BPLM	Big Person Little Mind
BR	Bathroom
BRB	Be Right Back
BRT	Be Right There
BS	Big Smile -or- Brain Strain
BSAAW	Big Smile And A Wink
BSBD&NE	Book Smart, Brain Dead &
....	No Experience
BSF	But Seriously, Folks
BSOD	Blue Screen of Death
BT	Byte This
BTA	But Then Again -or-
....	Before The Attacks
BTCOOM	Beats The Crap Out Of Me
BTDT	Been There Done That
BTDTGTS	Been There, Done That,
....	Got The T-shirt
BTHOOM	Beats The Heck Out Of Me
BTN	Better Than Nothing
BTOIYB	Be There Or It's Your Butt
BTTT	Back To The Top -or-
....	Bump To The Top

BTW	By The Way
BTWBO	Be There With Bells On
BTWITIAILW/U	By The Way I Think I Am In Love With You
B/W	Between
BW	Best Wishes
BWDIK	But What Do I Know
BWL	Bursting With Laughter
BWO	Black, White or Other
BY	Good Bye
BYKT	But you Knew That
BYOA	Bring Your Own Advil
BYOB	Bring Your Own Bottle -or- Bring Your Own Beer
BYOW	Build Your Own Website -or- Bring Your Own Wine
BZ	Busy

C

C&G	Chuckly and Grin
C-P	Sleepy
C-T	City
C/P	Cross Post
C/S	Change of Subject

C4N	Ciao For Now
CAAC	Cool As A Cucumber
CAS	Crack A Smile
CB	Chat Brat -or- Coffee Break
CBB	Can't Be Bothered
CD	Calm Down
CD9	Code 9 - it means parents are around
CEO	Chief Executive Officer
CF	Coffee Freak
CFV	Call For Vote
CIAO	Goodbye (in Italian)
CIBM	Could It Be Magic?
CICO	Coffee In, Coffee Out
CICYHW	Can I Copy Your Home Work
CID	Consider It Done -or- Crying In Disgrace
CIL	Check In Later
CIS	CompuServe Information Service
CLM	Career Limiting Move
CM	Call Me
CMBP	Cover My Butt Partner
CMF	Count My Fingers
CMIW	Correct Me if I'm Wrong

CMU	Crack Me Up
CNP	Continued in Next Post
CO	Chill Out
COB	Close Of Business
COD	Change Of Dressing
CofS	Church of Scientology
COS	Change Of Subject
CRAP	Cheap Redundant Assorted Products
CRAT	Can't Remember A Thing
CRB	Come Right Back
CRBT	Crying Real Big Tears
CRC	Can't Remember Crap
CRDTCHCK	Credit Check
CRTLA	Can't Remember the Three-Letter Acronym
CS	Career Suicide
CSA	Cool Sweet Awesome
CSL	Can't Stop Laughing
CSN	Chuckle, Snicker, Grin
CT	Can't Talk
CTA	Call To Action
CTC	Care To Chat
CTO	Check This Out

CU	See You -or- Cracking Up
CUATU	See You Around The Universe
CUL8R	See You Later
CULA	See You Later Alligator
CUNS	See You In School
CUPCK	Cupcake
CUOL	See You OnLine
CUWTA	Catch Up With The Acronyms
CUZ	Because
CWOT	Complete Waste Of Time
CWYL	Chat With You Later
CX	Cancelled
CY	Calm Yourself
CYA	See Ya
CYB	Call Your Boss
CYE	Check your Email
CYF	Call Your Father
CYL	See You Later
CYM	Check Your Mail -or- Call Your Mother
CYO	See You Online -or- Call Your Office
CYT	See You Tomorrow

D

D&M	Deep & Meaningful
DAK	Dead At Keyboard
DAMHIKT	Don't Ask Me How I Know That
DARFC	Ducking And Running For Cover
DBA	Doing Business As
DBD	Don't Be Dumb
DBEYR	Don't Believe Everything You Read
DD	Due Diligence -or- Double Down
DDD	Direct Distance Dial
DDSOC	Different Day, Same Old Crap
DEF	Definitely
DEGT	Don't Even Go There
DETI	Don't Even Think It
DF	Dear Friend
DFLA	Disenhanced Four-Letter Acronym (that is, a TLA)
DGA	Don't Go Anywhere
DGT	Don't Go There
DGTG	Don't Go There Girlfriend
DH	Dear Husband
DHYB	Don't Hold Your Breath
DIAF	Die In A Fire

DIC	Drunk In Charge
DIKU	Do I Know You
DILLIGAC	Do I Look Like I Give A Crap
DILLIGAD	Do I Look Like I Give A Darn
DINK	Double Incomes, No Kids
DIRFT	Do It Right the First Time
DISTO	Did I Say That Outloud?
DITR	Dancing In The Rain
DITYID	Did I Tell You I'm Distressed
DIY	Do It Yourself
DKDC	Don't Know Don't Care
DL	Download -or- Dead Link
DLTBBB	Don't Let The Bed Bugs Bite
DLTM	Don't Lie To Me
DMI	Don't Mention It
DNBL8	Do Not Be Late
DNC	Does Not Compute
DND	Do Not Disturb
DOA	Dead On Arrival
DOC	Drug Of Choice
DOE	Depends On Experience
DOEI	Goodbye (in Dutch)
DORD	Department Of Redundancy Dept.
DP	Domestic Partner

DPS	Damage Per Second
DPUP	Don't Poop Your Pants
DQMOT	Don't Quote Me On This
DQYDJ	Don't Quit Your Day Job
DRIB	Don't Read If Busy
DSTR8	Darn Straight
DTC	Deep Throaty Chuckle
DTRT	Do The Right Thing
DTTMN	Do Not Talk To Me Now
DUI	Driving Under the Influence
DUNA	Don't Use No Acronyms
DURS	Darn You Are Sexy
DUSL	Do You Scream Loud?
DUST	Did You See That
DWB	Don't Write Back
DWBH	Don't Worry Be Happy
DWI	Driving While Intoxicated
DWPKOTL	Deep Wet Passionate Kiss On The Lips
DWS	Driving While Stupid
DWWWI	Surfing the World Wide Web while intoxicated
DWYM	Does What You Mean
DYFM	Dude You Fascinate Me

DYHAB .... Do You Have A Boyfriend
DYHAG .... Do You Have A Girlfriend
DYJHIW .... Don't You Just Hate It When...
DYODW .... Do Your Own Dirty Work

E

E123 .... Easy as One, Two, Three
EAK .... Eating at Keyboard
EE .... Electronic Emission
EFT .... Electronic Funds Transfer
EG .... Evil Grin
EL .... Evil Laugh
EM .... Excuse Me
EMA .... E-Mail Address
EMFBI .... Excuse Me For Butting In
EMI .... Excuse My Ignorance
EML .... Email Me Later
EMRTW .... Evil Monkey's Rule The World
EMSG .... E-Mail Message
EOD .... End Of Day -or- End Of Discussion
EOL .... End Of Life
EOM .... End Of Message
EOT .... End Of Thread
EPAD .... Eat Poop And Die

EPADY..............	Eat Poop And Die You
ESEMED	Every Second Every Minute
....	Every Day
ESH	Experience, Strength, and Hope
ESO	Equipment Smarter than Operator
ETA................	Estimated Time of Arrival -or-
....	Edited To Add
EVRE1	Every One
EWI	E-mailing While Intoxicated
EZ....................	Easy

F

F2F	Face-to-Face
F2T	Free To Talk
FAB................	Features Attributes Benefits
FAQL	Frequently Asked Questions List
FAWC	For Anyone Who Cares
FAWOMT.........	Frequently Argued Waste Of
....	My Time
FBKS	Failure Between Keyboard
....	and Seat
FCFS	First Come, First Served
FDGB	Fall Down Go Boom
FE....................	Fatal Error

FF	Friends Forever
FF&PN	Fresh Fields and Pastures New
FGAI	Forget About It
FIL	Father-In-Law
FILTH	Failed In London, Try Hong Kong
FISH	First in, Still Here
FITB	Fill In The Blanks
FLA	Four Letter Acronym
FMTYEWTK	Far More Than You Ever Wanted To Know
FOAF	Friend Of A Friend
FOC	Free of Charge
FOC	Full Of Crap
FOFL	Falling on Floor Laughing
FOL	Fond of Leather
FOMC	Fell Off My Chair
FOMCL	Falling Off My Chair Laughing
FORD	Found On Road Dead -or- Fixed Or Repaired Daily
FPS	For Petes Sake
FS	For Sale
FSBO	For Sale By Owner
FSR	For Some Reason
FST	Fast

FTASB	Faster Than A Speeding Bullet
FTBOMH	From The Bottom Of My Heart
FTF	Face To Face
FTFOI	For The Fun Of It
FTL	Faster Than Light
FTLOG	For The Love Of God
FTR	For The Record
FTTB	For The Time Being
FTW	For The Win
FUD	Fear, Uncertainty, and Disinformation
FURTB	Filled Up and Ready To Burst
FWB	Friends With Benefits
FWD	Forward
FWIW	For What It's Worth
FYA	For Your Amusement
FYE	For Your Edification
FYEO	For Your Eyes Only
FYF	From your Friend
FYI	For Your Information
FYLTGE	From Your Lips To Gods Ears
FYM	For Your Misinformation
FYSBIGTBABN	Fasten Your SeatBelts It's Going To Be A Bumpy Night

G

GDW	Grin, Duck and Wave
GF	Girlfriend
GF	Go Figure
GFI	Go For It
GFN	Gone For Now
GFON	Good For One Night
GFR	Grim File Reaper
GFTD	Gone For The Day
GFY	Good For You -or-
	Go Find Yourself
GG	Good Game -or-
	Gotta Go
GGA	Good Game All
GGN	Gotta Go Now
GGOH	Gotta Get Out of Here
GGP	Gotta Go Pee
GI	Google It
GIC	Gift In Crib
GIDK	Gee I Don't Know
GIGO	Garbage In, Garbage Out
GIWIST	Gee, I Wish I'd Said That
GJ	Good Job
GJP	Good Job Partner
GL	Good Luck -or- Get Lost

GRRR	Growling
GSOH	Good Sense Of Humor
GT	Good Try
GTG	Got To Go
GTGB	Got To Go, Bye
GTGP	Got To Go Pee
GTHOOH	Get The Heck Out Of Here
GTK	Good To Know
GTM	Giggle To Myself
GTRM	Going To Read Mail
GTSY	Glad To See You
GUD	Geographically UnDesirable
GWI	Get With It
GWS	Get Well Soon
GYHOOYB	Get Your Head Out Of Your Butt

H

H&K	Hugs and Kisses
h/o	Hold On
h/p	Hold Please
H4U	Hot For You
H4XX0R	Hacker -or- To Be Hacked
H8	Hate
HAGD	Have a Great Day

HAGN.........Have A Good Night
HAGO.........Have A Good One
HAK.........Hugs And Kisses
hak/xoxo.........Hugs and Kisses
HAND.........Have a Nice Day
HAR.........Hit And Run
HAWTLW.........Hello And Welcome To Last Week
HAY.........How Are You
HB.........Hurry Back
HBASTD.........Hitting Bottom And Starting To Dig
HBB.........Hip Beyond Belief
HBIB.........Hot But Inappropriate Boy
HBU.........How Bout You?
HCC.........Holy Computer Crap
HD.........Hold
HF.........Hello Friend -or- Have Fun -or-
.........Have Faith
HHIS.........Hanging Head In Shame
HHO1/2K.........Ha Ha, Only Half Kidding
HHOJ.........Ha-Ha, Only Joking
HHOK.........Ha Ha, Only Kidding
HHOS.........Ha-Ha, Only Serious
HHTYAY.........Happy Holidays To You And Yours
HIG.........How's It Going

HIH	Hope It Helps
HIOOC	Help, I'm Out Of Coffee
HITAKS	Hang In There And Keep Smiling
HNTI	How Nice That/This Is
HNTW	How Nice That Was
HNY	Happy New Year
HO	Hang On -or- Hold On
HOH	House Of Hamburgers
HOHA	Hollywood Hacker
HOIC	Hold On, I'm Coming
HOYEW	Hanging On Your Every Word
HP	Higher Power
HPPO	Highest Paid Person in Office
HSIK	How Should I Know
HT	Hi There
HTH	Hope This (or That) Helps
HTNOTH	Hit The Nail On The Head
HUA	Heads Up Ace
HUGZ	Hugs
HWGA	Here We Go Again

I

I 1-D-R	I Wonder
I-D-L	Ideal

IAC	In Any Case -or-
	I Am Confused
IAE	In Any Event
IAITS	It's All In The Subject
IANAC	I Am Not A Crook
IANADBIPOOTV	I Am Not A Doctor But I Play
	One On TV
IANAE	I Am Not An Expert
IANAL	I Am Not A Lawyer
IANNNGC	I Am Not Nurturing the Next
	Generation of Casualties
IASAP4U	I Always Say A Prayer For You
IAT	I Am Tired
IAW	I Agree With -or-
	In Accordance With
IAYM	I Am Your Master
IBGYBG	I'll Be Gone, You'll Be Gone
IBIWISI	I'll Believe It When I See It
IBK	Idiot Behind Keyboard
IBRB	I'll Be Right Back
IBT	In Between Technology
IBTD	I Beg To Differ
IBTL	In Before The Lock
IC	Independant Contractor -or-
	In Character -or- I See

ICBW	I Could Be Wrong
ICYC	In Case You're Curious -or-
	In Case You Care
ID10T	Idiot
IDC	I Don't Care
IDGAD	I Don't Give A Darn
IDGI	I Don't Get It -or-
	I Don't Get Involved
IDK	I Don't Know
IDKY	I Don't Know You
IDM	It Does Not Matter
IDST	I Didn't Say That
IDTA	I Did That Already
IDTS	I Don't Think So
IF/IB	In the Front -or- In the Back
IFAB	I Found A Bug
IGGP	I Gotta Go Pee
IGTP	I Get The Point
IHA	I Hate Acronyms
IHAIM	I Have Another Instant Message
IHNO	I Have No Opinion
IHTFP	I Have Truly Found Paradise
IHU	I Hear You
IHY	I Hate You

......	Coffee/Crumbs/Coke On
ILICISCOMK	I Laughed, I Cried, I Spat/Spilt
ILA	I Love Acronyms
IKYABWAI	I Know You Are But What Am I?
IKY	I Know, Right?
IKWYM	I Know What You Mean
IKALOPLT	I Know A Lot Of People Like That
IK	I Know
IJWTS	I Just Want To Say
IJWTK	I Just Want To Know
IJPMP	I Just Peed My Pants
IIWM	If It Were Me
IITYWYBMAD	If I Tell You Will You
......	Buy Me A Drink
IIYWIMWYBMAD	If I Tell You What It Means Will
......	You Buy Me A Drink
IILTYTO	If It's Too Loud You're Too Old
IIT	Is It Tight?
......	If I Recall Correctly
IIRC	I Remember Correctly -or-
IIRif	I Remember -or- If I Recall
IIMAD	If It Makes An(y) Difference
OIIO	Intel Inside, Idiot Outside
IIABDFI	If It Ain't Broke, Don't Fix It

ILU	I Love You
ILUAAF	I Love You As A Friend
ILY	I Love You
ILYSM	I Love You So Much
IM	Instant Messaging -or-
	Immediate Message
IM2BZ2P	I aM Too Busy To (even) Pee
IMA	I Might Add
IMAO	In My Arrogant Opinion
IMCO	In My Considered Opinion
IMDB	Internet Movie Database
IME	In My Experience
IMHEIUO	In My High Exalted Informed
	Unassailable Opinion
IMHO	In My Humble Opinion
IMNERHO	In My Never Even Remotely
	Humble Opinion
IMNSHO	In My Not So Humble Opinion
IMO	In My Opinion
IMOO	In My Own Opinion
IMPOV	In My Point Of View
IMRU	I Am, Are You?
IMS	I Am Sorry

INBD	It's No Big Deal
INMP	It's Not My Problem
INNW	If Not Now, When
INPO	In No Particular Order
INUCOSM	It's No Use Crying Over Spilt Milk
IOH	I'm Outta Here
ION	Index Of Names
IOUD	Inside, Outside, Upside Down
IOW	In Other Words
IRL	In Real Life
ISAGN	I See A Great Need
ISH	Insert Sarcasm Here
ISO	In Search Of
ISS	I Said So -or- I'm So Sure
ISSYGTI	I'm So Sure You Get The Idea
ISTM	It Seems to Me
ISTR	I Seem To Remember
ISWYM	I See What You Mean
ISYALS	I'll Send You A Letter Soon
ITA	I Totally Agree
ITFA	In The Final Analysis
ITIGBS	I Think I'm Going To Be Sick
ITM	In The Money

ITSFWI	If The Shoe Fits Wear It
IUM	If You Must
IWALU	I Will Always Love You
IWBAPTAKYBIYSTA	I Will Buy A Plane Ticket And Kick Your Butt If You Say That Again
IWBNI	It Would Be Nice If
IWIWU	I Wish I Was You
IYD	In Your Dreams
IYKWIM	If You Know What I Mean
IYKWIMAITYD	If You Know What I Mean And I Think You Do
IYO	In Your Opinion
IYQ	I Like You
IYSS	If You Say So
IYSWIM	If You See What I Mean

J

J/C	Just Checking
J/J	Just Joking
J/K	Just Kidding
J/P	Just Playing
J/W	Just Wondering

JZLYK......Just To Let You Know
J4F......Just For Fun
J4G......Just For Grins
J4T or JFT......Just For Today
J5M......Just Five Minutes
JAD......Just Another day
JAS......Just A Salesman
JAM......Just A Minute
JAS......Just A Second
JC......Just Curious -or- Just Chilling
JDI......Just Do It
JFI......Just For Information
JIC......Just In Case
JK......Just Kidding
JM2C......Just My 2 Cents
JMO......Just My Opinion
JOOTT......Just One Of Those Things
JP......Just Playing
JSU......Just Shut Up
JSYK......Just So You Know
JT......Just Teasing
JLTYK......Just To Let You Know
JTOL......Just Thinking Out Loud
JTOU......Just Thinking Of You

JUADLAM	Jumping Up And Down
	Like A Monkey
JW	Just Wondering

K

K	Okay
KK	Okay
OK	Okay
KB	Kick Butt
KBD	Keyboard
KFY -or- K4Y	Kiss For You
KHYF	Know How You Feel
KIA	Killed In Action
KIBO	Knowledge In, Bullcrap Out
KIR	Keep It Real
KISS	Keep It Simple Stupid
KIT	Keep In Touch
KK	Kiss Kiss
KMB	Kiss My Butt
KMP	Keep Me Posted
KMUF	Kiss Me You Fool
KOK	Knock
KOTC	Kiss On The Cheek
KOTL	Kiss On The Lips

KPC .... Keeping Parents Clueless
KUTGW .... Keep Up The Good Work
KWIM .... Know What I Mean?
KYFC .... Keep Your Fingers Crossed
KYPO .... Keep Your Pants On

L

L .... Laugh
L8R .... Later
LBR and LGR .... Little Boy's Room,Little Girl's Room
LD .... Long Distance -or- Later Dude
LDL .... Let's Discuss Live
LDIMEDILUGAC .... Look Deeply Into My Eyes, Does it Look Like I Give A Crap
LDR .... Long Distance Relationship
LDTTWA .... Let's Do The Time Warp Again
LFTI .... Looking Forward To It
LG .... Lovely Greetings
LGMAS .... Lord Give Me A Sign
LHO .... Laughing Head Off
LIFO .... Last In, First Out
LIS .... Laughing In Silence
LJBF .... Let's Just Be Friends
LKITR .... Little Kid in The Room

LLC	Lady Looking Cool
LLTA	Lots and Lots of Thunderous Applause
LMBO	Laughing My Butt Off
LMHO	Laughing My Head Off
LMIRL	Let's Meet In Real Life
LMK	Let Me Know
LMSO	Laughing My Socks Off
LMTCB	Left Message To Call Back
LOL	Laughing Out Loud -or- Lots of Love
LOLA	Laugh Out Loud Again
LOML	Love Of My Life
LONH	Lights On, Nobody Home
LOOL	Laughing Outrageously Out Loud
LOPSOD	Long On Promises, Short On Delivery
LOU	Laughing Over You
LPOC	Lazy Piece Of Crap
LRF	Little Rubber Feet
LSHMBH	Laughing So Hard My Belly Hurts
LTHTT	Laughing Too Hard To Type
LTIC	Laughing 'Til I Cry

LTM	Laughing To Myself
LTNS	Long Time No See
LTNT	Long Time, No Type
LTR	Long Term Relationship
LTS	Laughing to Self
LTTIC	Look, The Teacher Is Coming
LULU	Locally Undesireable Land Use
LUMTP	Love You More Than Pie
LUSM	Love You So Much
LWR	Launch When Ready
LY	Love You
LY4E	Love You Forever
LYA	Love You All
LYB	Love You Babe
LYCYLBB	Love You, See You Later, Bye Bye
LYKYAMY	Love You, Kiss You, Already Miss You
LYL	Love You Lots
LYLAB	Love You Like a Brother
LYLAS	Love You Like A Sister
LYLB	Love You Later Bye
LYMI	Love You, Mean It
LYWAMH	Love You With All My Heart

M

M2NY	Me Too, Not Yet
M4C	Meet for Coffee
M8 or M8s	Mate -or- Mates
MA	Mature Audience
MAYA	Most Advanced Yet Accessible
MB	Message Board
MBN	Must Be Nice
MBRN	Must Be Real Nice
MCIBTY	My Computer Is Better Than Yours
MEGO	My Eyes Glaze Over
MFD	Multi-Function Device
MHBFY	My Heart Bleeds For You
MHDC	My Hard Disk Crashed
MHOTY	My Hat's Off To You
MIA	Missing In Action
MIHAP	May I Have Your Attention Please
MIL	Mother-In-Law
MIRL	Meet In Real Life
MITIN	More Info Than I Needed
MKOP	My Kind Of Place

MLA	Multiple Letter Acronym
MLAS	My Lips Are Sealed
MLF	My Love Forever
MLOS	Mom Looking Over Shoulder
MM	Market Maker
MMHA2U	My Most Humble Apologies To You
MO	Move On
MOF	Matter Of Fact
MOMPL	One Moment Please
MOO	Matter Of Opinion
MOP	Moment Please
MorF	Male or Female
MOS	Mom Over Shoulder
MOSS	Member(s) Of The Same Sex
MOTAS	Member Of The Appropriate Sex
MOTD	Message Of The Day
MOTOS	Member(s) Of The Opposite Sex
MOTSS	Member(s) Of The Same Sex
MRA	Moving Right Along
MRPH	Mail the Right Place for Help
MSG	Message
MSMD	Monkey See Monkey Do

MTBF	Mean Time Before Failure
MTF	More To Follow
MTFBWY	May The Force Be With You
MTLA	My True Love Always
MTSBWY	May The Schwartz Be With You
MUBAR	Messed up Beyond All Recognition
MUSM	Miss You So Much
MWBRL	More Will Be Revealed Later
MYL	Mind Your Language
MYOB	Mind Your Own Business

N

N/A	Not Applicable -or- Not Affiliated
N/M	Nothing Much
N/T	No Text
N1	Nice One
N2M	Not To Mention -or- Not Too Much
N2MJCHBU	Not Too Much Just Chillin, How Bout You?
NAB	Not A Blonde
NADT	Not A Darn Thing
NAGB	Nearly Almost A Good Bridge
NAK	Nursing At Keyboard
NALOPKT	Not A Lot Of People Know That

NAVY	Never Again Volunteer Yourself
NAZ	Name, Address, Zip (also means Nasdaq)
NB4T	Not Before Time
NBD	No Big Deal
NBFAB	Not Bad For A Beginner
NBIF	No Basis In Fact
NBLFY	Nothing But Love For You
NC	Nice Crib
NCG	New College Graduate
NDN	Indian -or- Native American
NE	Anyway
NE1	Anyone
NE14KFC	Anyone for KFC?
NE1ER	Anyone Here
Ne2H	Need To Have
NESEC	Any Second
NETMA	Nobody Ever Tells Me Anything
NEV	Neighborhood Electric Vehicle
NEWS	North, East, West, South
NFBSK	Not For British School Kids
NFC	Not Favorably Considered
NFS	Not For Sale
NFW	No Feasible Way
NG	Not Good

NG	New Game
NGB................	Nearly Good Bridge
NH	Nice Hand
NHOH.............	Never Heard Of Him/Her
NI.....................	No Idea
NICE................	Nonsense In Crappy Existence
NIGYYSOG	Now I've Got You, You Son
....	Of a Gun
NIH	Not Invented Here
NIM..................	No Internal Message
NIMBY	Not In My Back Yard
NIMJD	Not In My Job Description
NIMQ...............	Not In My Queue
NIMY	Never In A Million Years
NINO	Nothing In, Nothing Out -or-
....	No Input, No Output
NISM	Need I Say More
NITL................	Not In This Lifetime
NIYWD	Not In Your Wildest Dreams
NLL..................	Nice Little Lady
NM...................	Never Mind -or- Nothing Much
....	-or- Nice Move
NME	Enemy
NMH	Not Much Here

NMHJC	Not Much Here, Just Chilling
NMP	Not My Problem
NMTE	Now More Than Ever
NMU	Not Much, You?
NN	Not Now
NNCIMIMINTZ	Not Now Chief, I'm In The Zone
NNWWW	Nudge, Nudge, Wink, Wink
ON	Not Online
NOA	Not Online Anymore
NOFI	No Offence Intended
NOS	New Old Stock
NOY	Not Online Yet
NOYB	None Of Your Business
NP	No Problem -or- Nosy Parents
NQA	No Questions Asked
NQOCD	Not Quite Our Class Dear
NR	Nice Roll
NRG	Energy
NRN	No Reply Necessary
NSA	No Strings Attached
NSFW	Not Safe For Work
NSTLC	Need Some Tender Loving Care
NTA	Not This Again
NTRTL	Not To Be Taken Literally

NTIM	Not That It Matters
NTIMM	Not That It Matters Much
NTK	Nice To Know
NTM	Not That Much
NTTAWWT	Not That There's Anything Wrong With That
NTW	Not To Worry
NTYMI	Now That You Mention It
NUB	New person to a site or game
NUFF	Enough Said
NVM	Never Mind
NVNG	Nothing Ventured, Nothing Gained
NW	No Way
NWAL	Nerd Without A Life
NWR	Not Work Related
NYC	Not Your Concern

O

O	Opponent -or- Over
OAO	Over And Out
OATUS	On A Totally Unrelated Subject
OAUS	On An Unrelated Subject
OB	Obligatory
OBE	Overcome By Events

OBO	Or Best Offer
OBTW	Oh By The Way
OBX	Old Battle Axe
OC	Original Character -or-
	Own Character
OCD	Obsessive Compulsive Disorder
OCIF	Oh Crap I Forgot
OCINTOT	Oh Crap I Never
	Thought Of That
ODTAA	One Darn Thing After Another
OIC	Oh, I See
OICU812	Oh I See, You Ate One Too
OK	All Correct
OL	Old Lady
OLL	OnLine Love
OLN	OnLine Netiquette
OM	Old Man
OMB	Oh My Buddha
OMDB	Over My Dead Body
OMG	Oh My God
OMIK	Open Mouth, Insert Keyboard
OML	Oh My Lord
OMW	On My Way
ONID	Oh No I Didn't

ONNA	Oh No, Not Again
ONNTA	Oh No, Not This Again
ONUD	Oh No You Didn't
OO	Over and Out
OOAK	One Of A Kind
OOC	Out Of Character -or-
	Out Of Control
OOF	Out Of Facility
OOI	Out Of Interest
OOO	Out Of Office
OOS	Out Of Stock
OOTB	Out Of The Box -or-
	Out Of The Blue
OOTC	Obligatory On Topic Comment
OST	On Second Thought
OT	Off Topic
OTASOIC	Owing To A Slight Oversight
	In Construction
OTC	Over The Counter
OTF	Off The Floor -or-
	On The phone (Fone)
OTH	Off The Hook
OTL	Out To Lunch
OTOH	On The Other Hand

OTP	On The Phone
OTT	Over The Top
OTTOMH	Off The Top Of My Head
OTW	Off The Wall
OUSU	Oh, You Shut Up
OWTTE	Or Words To That Effect
OZ	Australia

P

P	Partner
P&C	Private & Confidential
P-ZA	Pizza
P2C2E	Process Too Complicated Too Explain
P2U4URAQTP	Peace To You For You Are A Cutie Pie
P911	Parent Alert
PA	Parent Alert
PAL	Parents Are Listening
PANS	Pretty Awesome New Stuff
PASS	Pull, Aim, Squeeze, Sweep
PAW	Parents Are Watching
PB	Potty Break
PBB	Parent Behind Back

PBEM	Play By EMail
PBJ	Peanut Butter and Jelly
PC	Personal Computer -or-
	Politically Correct
PCM	Please Call Me
PD	Public Domain
PDA	Public Display of Affection
PDQ	Pretty Darn Quick
PDS	Please Don't Shout
PEBCAC	Problem Exists Between
	Chair And Computer
PEBCAK	Problem Exists Between Chair
	And Keyboard
PEEP	People Engaged and
	Empowered for Peace
PFA	Please Find Attached
PFM	Please Forgive Me
PHB	Pointy Haired Boss
PHS	Pointy Haired Stupidvisor
PIAPS	Pig In A Pant Suit
PIBKAC	Problem Is Between Keyboard
	And Chair
PICNIC	Problem In Chair, Not In Computer
PIF	Paid In Full

PIMP	Peeing In My Pants
PIMPL	Peeing In My Pants Laughing
PIN	Person In Need
PIR	Parent In Room
PLO	Peace, Love, Out
PLOKTA	Press Lots Of Keys To Abort
PLOS	Parents Looking Over Shoulder
PLS	Please
PLZ	Please
PM	Personal Message -or-
	Private Message
PMBI	Pardon My Butting In
PMF	Pardon My French -or-
	Pure Freaking Magic
PMFJI	Pardon Me For Jumping In
PMIGBOM	Put Mind In Gear Before
	Opening Mouth
PMJI	Pardon My Jumping In
PMP	Peeing My Pants
PMSL	Peed MySelf Laughing
PNATMBC	Pay No Attention To Man Behind
	the Curtain
PNCAH	Please, No Cursing
	Allowed Here

PND	Possibly Not Definitely -or-
	Personal Navigation Device
PO	Peed Off
POAHF	Put On A Happy Face
POAK	Passed Out At Keyboard
POCC	Piece Of Crap Computer
POMS	Parent Over My Shoulder
PONA	Person Of No Account
POOF	Good-bye, gone; also seen as
POS	Parent Over Shoulder
POTS	Plain Old Telephone System -or-
	Pat On The Shoulder
POTUS	President of the United States
POTW	Project Of The Week
POV	Point of View
POW	Prisoner Of War
PP	People
PPL	Pay-Per-Lead -or- People
PRW	Parents Are Watching
PS	Post Script
PSA	Public Service Announcement
PSO	Product Superior to Operator
PTH	Prime Tanning Hours
PTMM	Please Tell Me More

PTP .... Pardon The Pun

PU .... That Stinks

PUK .... Pick Up Kids

PVP .... Player Versus Player

PWN .... Own

PWNT .... Owned

PWP .... Plot, What Plot?

Q

QFT .... Quoted For Truth

QL .... Quit Laughing

QLS .... Reply

QOTD .... Quote Of The Day

QQ .... Quick Question -or-
Cry More

QS .... Quit Scrolling

QT .... Cutie

R

R U .... Are you there?

R&D .... Research & Development

R&R .... Rest & Relaxation

RAEBNC .... Read And Enjoyed,
But No Comment

RB@Ya	Right Back at Ya
RBAY	Right Back At You
RBTL	Read Between The Lines
RC	Remote Control
RE	Regards -or- Reply -or-
	Hello Again
REHI	Hi Again
RFD	Request For Discussion
RGR	Roger
RHIP	Rank Has Its Privileges
RIYL	Recommended If You Like
RKBA	Right to Keep and Bear Arms
RL	Real Life
RLCO	Real Life Conference
RLF	Real Life Friend
RM	Remake
RMLB	Read My Lips Baby
RMMA	Reading My Mind Again
RMMM	Read My Mail Man
RN	Right Now
RNN	Reply Not Necessary
ROFL	Rolling On Floor Laughing
ROTFL	Rolling On The Floor Laughing

ROTFLMBO	Rolling On The Floor Laughing My Butt Off
ROTFLOL	Rolling On The Floor Laughing Out Loud
ROTGL	Rolling On The Ground Laughing
ROTGLMBO	Rolling On The Ground Laughing My Butt Off
ROTM	Right On The Money
RPG	Role Playing Games
RR	Really Rich
RRQ	Return Receipt Request
RS	Really Soon
RSN	Real Soon Now
RSVP	Répondez S'il Vous Plaît
RT	Real Time
RTBM	Read The Bloody Manual
RTBS	Reason To Be Single
RTFAQ	Read The FAQ
RTQ	Read The Question
RTH	Release The Hounds
RTK	Return To Keyboard
RTM	Read The Manual
RTSM	Read The Silly Manual
RTSD	Right Thing To Say Dude

RTWQ	Read The Whole Question
RU	Are You?
RU/18	Are You Over 18?
RUKM	Are You Kidding Me?
RUMCYMHMD	Are You on Medication Cause You Must Have Missed a Dose
RUMORF	Are You Male OR Female?
RUNTS	Are You Nuts?
RUOK	Are You OK?
RUS	Are You Serious?
RUSOS	Are You SOS (in trouble)?
RUT	Are You There?
RUUP4IT	Are You Up For It?
RX	Regards
RYFM	Read Your Friendly Manual
RYO	Roll Your Own
RYS	Read Your Screen

S

S	Smile
S2R	Send To Receive
S2U	Same To You
S4L	Spam For Life

SAHM	Stay At Home Mom
SAPFU	Surpassing All Previous Foul Ups
SB	Stand By
SBI	Sorry 'Bout It
SBTA	Sorry, Being Thick Again
SBUG	Small Bald Unaudacious Goal
SCNR	Sorry, Could Not Resist
SCOB	Spilled Coffee On Book
SDK	Scottie Doesn't Know -or- Software Developer's Kit
SEC	Wait a second
SED	Said Enough Darling
SEP	Somebody Else's Problem
SETE	Smiling Ear To Ear
SEWG	Scientifically Engineered Wild Guess
SF	Surfer Friendly -or- Science Fiction
SFAIAA	So Far As I Am Aware
SFETE	Smiling From Ear To Ear
SFLA	Stupid Four Letter Acronym
SFX	Sound Effects -or- Stage Effects
SH	Stuff Happens
SHB	Should Have Been

SHID	Slap Head In Disgust
SHMILY	See How Much I Love You
SIC	Spelling Is Correct
SICL	Sitting In Chair Laughing
SICS	Sitting In Chair Snickering
SII	Seriously Impaired Imagination
SIL	Sister-In-Law
SIP	Skiing In Powder
SIT	Stay In Touch
SITCOMs	Single Income, Two Children, Oppressive Mortgage
SITD	Still In The Dark
SITSL	Sorry I Took So Long
Sk8r	Skater
SL	Second Life
SLAP	Sounds Like A Plan
SLAW	Sounds Like A Winner
SLF	Sounds Like Fun
SLIRK	Smart Little Rich Kid
SLM	See Last Mail
SLOM	Sticking Leeches On Myself
SLT	Something Like That
SM	Senior Moment
SMAIM	Send Me An Instant Message

SME	Subject Matter Expert
SMEM	Send Me E-Mail
SMH	Shaking My Head
SMIM	Send Me an Instant Message
SMOP	Small Matter of Programming
SNAFU	Situation Normal, All Fouled Up
SNAG	Sensitive New Age Guy
SNERT	Snotty Nosed Egotistical Rotten Teenager
SO	Significant Other
SOBT	Stressed Out Big Time
SOH	Sense Of Humor
SOHF	Sense Of Humor Failure
SOI	Self Owning Idiot
SOI	Sit On It
SOMY	Sick Of Me Yet
SOP	Standard Operating Procedure
SOS	Same Old Stuff
SOSDD	Same Old Stuff Different Day
SOT	Short On Time
SOTMG	Short On Time, Must Go
SOW	Speaking Of Which -or- Statement Of Work

SOZ	Sorry
SPYNGTW	Stop Picking Your Nose, Get To Work
SRO	Standing Room Only
SRSLY	Seriously
SRY	Sorry
SSC	Super Sexy Cute
SSDD	Same Stuff Different Day
SSEWBA	Someday Soon, Everything Will Be Acronyms
SSIA	Subject Says It All
STBY	Sucks To Be You
STD	Seal The Deal
STHU	Shut The Heck Up
STTM	Stop Talking To Me
STW	Search The Web
STR8	Straight
STS	So To Speak
STW	Search The Web
STYS	Speak To You Soon
SU	Shut Up
SUAKM	Shut Up And Kiss Me
SUFID	Screwing Up Face In Disgust
SUL	Snooze You Lose

SUP .... What's Up?
SUYF .... Shut Up You Fool
SWAK .... Sealed (or Sent) With A Kiss
SWALBCAKWS .... Sealed With A Lick Because A Kiss Won't Stick
SWALK .... Sealed With A Loving Kiss
SWDYT .... So What Do You Think
SWF .... Single White Female
SWIM .... See What I Mean?
SWIS .... See What I'm Saying
SWL .... Screaming With Laughter
SWMBO .... She Who Must Be Obeyed
SWU .... So What's Up
SYS .... See You Soon
SYT .... See You Tomorrow
Sv .... What's Up?

T

T&C .... Terms & Conditions
T@YL .... Talk At You Later
TA .... Thanks Again
TAF .... That's All, Folks!
TAFN .... That's All For Now
TAH .... Take A Hike

TAKS	That's A Knee Slapper
TANJ	There Ain't No Justice
TANSTAAFL	There Ain't No Such Thing As A Free Lunch
TAP	Take A Pill
TARSU	Things Are Really Screwd Up
TAS	Taking A Shower
TAW	Teachers Are Watching
TBA	To Be Advised
TBC	To Be Continued
TBD	To Be Determined
TBE	Thick Between Ears
TBH	To Be Honest
TBYB	Try Before You Buy
TC	Take Care
TCB	Trouble Came Back
TCFW	Too Cute For Words
TCOB	Taking Care Of Business
TCOY	Take Care Of Yourself
TCS	Take Care Sweetheart
TDM	Too Darn Many
TDTML	Talk Dirty To Me Later
TEOTWAWKI	The End Of The World As We Know It

TFDS	That is For Darn Sure
TFLMS	Thanks For Letting Me Share
TFN	Thanks For Nothing -or-
	Til Further Notice
TFS	Thanks For Sharing -or-
	Three Finger Salute
TFTHAOT	Thanks For The Help Ahead Of Time
TFTT	Thanks For The Thought
TFX	Traffic
TGAL	Think Globally, Act Locally
TGGTG	That Girl/Guy has Got To Go
TGIF	Thank God It's Friday
THX or TX or THKS	Thanks
TIA	Thanks In Advance
TIAIL	Think I Am In Love
TIC	Tongue In Cheek
TIGAD	Think I Give A Darn
TILII	Tell It Like It Is
TINWIS	That Is Not What I Said
TISC	This Is So Cool
TISL	This Is So Lame
TISNC	This Is So Not Cool

TISNF	That Is So Not Fair
TISNT	That Is So Not True
TK	To Come
TKU4UK	Thank You For Your Kindness
TLA	Three Letter Acronym
TLC	Tender Loving Care
TLGO	The List Goes On
TLITBC	That's Life In The Big City
TLK-2-U-L-8-R	Talk To You Later
TLTR	Too Long To Read
TM	Trust Me
TMA	Too Many Acronyms
TMI	Too Much Information
TMIU	The Manual Is Unreadable
TMTOWTDI	There's More Than One Way To Do It
TNA	Temporarily Not Available
TNC	Tongue In Cheek
TNT	Til Next Time
TNTL	Trying Not To Laugh
TNX	Thanks
TOA	Text On Arrival
TOBAL	There Oughta Be A Law
TOBG	This Oughta Be Good

TTKSF	Trying To Keep a Straight Face
TTS	Text To Speech
TTT	That's The Ticket -or- To The Top -or- Thought That Too
TTTHTFAL	Talk To The Hand, The Face Ain't Listening
TTTKB	Time To Totally Kick Butt
TTTT	To Tell The Truth
TTUL	Talk To You Later
TTYAWFN	Talk To You A While From Now
TTYL	Talk To You Later -or- Type To You Later
TTYS	Talk To You Soon
TTYT	Talk To You Tomorrow
TVM4YEM	Thank You Very Much For Your E-Mail
TVN	Thank You Very Much
TWHAB	This Won't Hurt A Bit
TWIMC	To Whom it may Concern
TWIWI	That Was Interesting, Wasn't It?
TXS	Thanks
TXT	Text
TXT IM	Text Instant Message
TY	Thank You

TYCLO .... Turn Your CAPS LOCK Off
TYSM .... Thank You So Much
TYVM .... Thank You Very Much

U

U .... You
U-L .... You Will
U2 .... You Too
U8 .... You Ate?
UBS .... Unique Buying State
UCWAP .... Up a Creek Without A Paddle
UDH82BME .... You'd Hate To Be Me
UG2BK .... You've Got To Be Kidding
UGC .... User-Generated Content
UNTCO .... You Need To Chill Out
UOK .... Are You OK?
UPOD .... Under Promise Over Deliver
UR .... You Are
UR2K .... You Are Too Kind
URAPITB .... You Are A Pain In The Butt
URSAI .... You Are Such An Idiot
URTWFAM .... You Are Too Wise For Me
URW .... You Are Welcome
URWS .... You Are Wise?

US	You Suck
USP	Unique Selling Proposition
UTM	You Tell Me
UV	Unpleasant Visual
UWIWU	You Wish I Was You

V

VBG	Very Big Grin
VBS	Very Big Smile
VC	Venture Capital
VCDA	Vaya Con Dios, Amigo
VEG	Very Evil Grin
VFM	Value For Money
VGN	Vegan -or- Vegitarian
VM	Voice Mail
VSF	Very Sad Face
VWD	Very Well Done
VWP	Very Well Played

W

W/	With
W/O	Without
W8	Wait
W84M	Wait For Me

WAD	Without A Doubt
WAEF	When All Else Fails
WAFS	Warm And Fuzzies
WAI...............	What An Idiot
WAK	What A Kiss
WAM...............	What A Mess
WAMBAM........	Web Application Meets Brick
....	And Mortar
WAY...............	Where Are You?
WAYD	What Are You Doing?
WAYN	Where Are You Now?
WB...................	Welcome Back -or- Write Back
WBS	Write Back Soon
WC...................	Who Cares
WCA	Who Cares Anyway
WD	Well Done
WDALYIC	Who Died And Left
....	You In Charge?
WDDD	Woopie Doo Da Dey
WDR...............	With Due Respect
WDT	Who Does That?
WDYM	What Do You Mean?
WDYMBT.........	What Do You Mean By That?
WDYS..............	What Did You Say

WDYT	What Do You Think
WE	Whatever
WEG	Wicked Evil Grin
WF	Way Fun
WFM	Works For Me
WG	Wicked Grin
WIBAMU	Well, I'll Be A Monkey's Uncle
WIBNI	Wouldn't It Be Nice If
WIIFM	What's In It For Me
WILCO	Will Comply
WIM	Woe Is Me
WIP	Work In Process
WISP	Winning Is So Pleasureable
WIT	Wordsmith In Training
WITW	What In The World
WIU	Wrap It Up
WL	White Lies
WMHGB	Where Many Have Gone Before
WMMOWS	Wash My Mouth Out With Soap
WMPL	Wet My Pants Laughing
WNOHGB	Where No One Has Gone Before
WOA	Work Of Art
WOG	Wise Old Guy

WOM	Word Of Mouse
WOMBAT	Waste Of Money, Brains And Time
WOOF	Well Off Older Folks
WOP	With Out Papers
WOTAM	Waste Of Time And Money
WOTD	Word Of The Day
WP	Well Played
WRT	With Regard To -or- With Respect To
WRUD	What Are You Doing?
WRUDATM	What Are You Doing At The Moment?
WT	Without Thinking -or- What The -or- Who The
WTB	Want To Buy
WTCHTF	When The Crap Hits The Fan
WTF	What The Frack
WTG	Way To Go
WTGFAD	Want To Go For A Drink?
WTGP	Want To Go Private?
WTH	What The Heck
WTHDTM	What The Heck Does That Mean?

WTHDYJS?	What The Heck Did You Just Say?
WTMI	Way Too Much Information
WTN	What Then Now? -or-
	Who Then Now?
WTS	Want To Sell
WTSDS	Where The Sun Don't Shine
WTTM	Without Thinking Too Much
WU	What's Up
WUF	Where You From
WUWH	Wish You Were Here
WUWHIMA	Wish You Were Here In My Arms
WWJD	What Would Jesus Do?
WWY	Where Were You?
WX	Weather
WYCM	Will You Call Me?
WYGISWYPF	What You Get Is What You Pay For
WYM	What do You Mean?
WYP	What's Your Problem?
WYRN	What's Your Real Name?
WYS	Whatever You Say
WYSIWYG	What You See Is What You Get
WYSLPG	What You See Looks
	Pretty Good

WYT .... Whatever You Think
WYWH .... Wish You Were Here

X

X-1-10 .... Exciting
XLNT .... Excellent
XME .... Excuse Me
XOXO .... Hugs and Kisses
XQZT .... Exquisite

Y

Y .... Why?
YA .... Yet Another
YABA .... Yet Another Bloody Acronym
YACC .... Yet Another Calendar Company
YAFIYGI .... You Asked For It You Got It
YAOTM .... Yet Another Off Topic Message
YAUN .... Yet Another Unix Nerd
YBS .... You'll Be Sorry
YBY .... Yeah Baby Yeah
YCT .... Your Comment To
YDKM .... You Don't Know Me

YEPPIES	Young Experimenting Perfection Seekers
YGBK	You Gotta Be Kidding
YGLT	You're Gonna Love This
YGTBK	You've Got To Be Kidding
YGWYPF	You Get What You Pay For
YHM	You Have Mail
YIC	Yours In Christ
YIU	Yes, I Understand
YIWGP	Yes, I Will Go Private
YKW	You Know What?
YKWIM	You Know What I Mean
YM	Your Mother
YMAK	You May Already Know
YMMV	Your Mileage May Vary
YNK	You Never Know
YOYO	You're On Your Own
YR	Yeah Right
YRYOCC	You're Running on Your Own Cookoo Clock
YS	You Stinker
YSAN	You're Such A Nerd
YSIC	Why Should I Care?

YSK .... You Should Know
YSYD .... Yeah, Sure You Do
YT .... You There?
YTB .... You're The Best
YTRNW .... Yeah That's Right, Now What?
YTTT .... You Telling The Truth?
YUPPIES .... Young Urban Professionals
YW .... You're Welcome
YWIA .... You're Welcome In Advance
YY4U .... Too Wise For You
YYSSW .... Yeah Yeah Sure Sure Whatever

Z

ZMG .... Oh My God
ZZZ .... Sleeping, Bored, Tired
\M/ .... Heavy Metal Music
^5 .... High Five
^RUP^ .... Read Up Please

SENIOR ADDENDUM

ATD .... At The Doctor's

BFF .... Best Friend Fell

BTW............... Bring The Wheelchair

BYOT .... Bring Your Own Teeth

CBM............... Covered By Medicare

CGU .... Can't Get Up

CRS .... Can't Remember Stuff

CUATSC .... See You At The Senior Center

DWI............... Driving While Incontinent

FWBB .... Friend With Beta Blockers

FWIW .... Forgot Where I Was

FYI .... Found Your Insulin

GGLKI .... Gotta Go, Laxative Kicking In

GGPBL........... Gotta Go, Pacemaker Battery Low!

GHA .... Got Heartburn Again

HGBM............ Had Good Bowel Movement

IMHO	Is My Hearing-Aid On?
LMDO	Laughing My Dentures Out
LMGA	Lost My Glasses Again
LOL	Living On Lipitor
LWO	Lawrence Welk's On
OMMR	On My Massage Recliner
OMSG	Oh My! Sorry, Gas.
ROFLACGU	Rolling On The Floor Laughing And Can't Get Up
SGGP	Sorry, Gotta Go Poop
TOT	Texting On Toilet
TTYL	Talk To You Louder
WAITT	Who Am I Talking To?
WNO	Wheelchair Needs Oil
WTFA	Wet The Furniture Again
WTP	Where's The Prunes?
WWNO	Walker Wheels Need Oil

NOTES

NOTES